D1672675

THE RHINO GATE POEMS

The Rhino Gate Poems

George Ellenbogen

SIGNAL EDITIONS IS AN IMPRINT OF VEHICULE PRESS MONTREAL CANADA

I would like to ackmowledge with thanks the indulgence of my editor, Michael Harris; the understanding of my publisher, Simon Dardick; the many critical suggestions of Evelyn Shakir; the varied attentions to the manuscript by Joan Oliveri, and the time and resources given to me by Bentley College, the Virginia Center for the Creative Arts, and the Whiting Foundation. Finally, a chorus of thanks to my brother, Irving Ellenbogen, for his ink sketches, which are part of the countertext in "The Rhino Gate."

Some of these poems have appeared in the following periodicals and anthologies: *Chelsea Hotel* (Germany), *Fiddlehead*, *Matrix*, *Parchment*, *Prairie Fire*, *Kaimana*, *Zymergy*, *Canadian Author and Bookman*

Published with the assistance of The Canada Council

Signal Editions series editor: Michael Harris
Cover art and design: Mark Garland
Typeset in Perpetua by Simon Garamond
Photograph of the author: Marcus Alonso
Printed by Imprimerie d'Édition Marquis Ltée

Copyright © George Ellenbogen 1996
All rights reserved.
Dépôt légal, Bibliothèque nationale du Québec and the National Library of Canada, second quarter 1996.

Cataloguing in Publication Data

Ellenbogen, George, 1934-
  The Rhino gate poems

ISBN 1-55065-079-3

1. Title.

PS8559.L542R48 1966   C811'.54   C96-900244-0
PR9199.3.E43R48 1996

Published by Véhicule Press, P.O.B. 125, Place du Parc Station, Montreal, Quebec, Canada H2W 2M9

Printed in Canada on alkaline paper.

For Evelyn
who reread
with insight and patience

Contents

The Rhino Gate

The phrase—"The Rhino Gate"—comes as an enigma that possesses the narrator of this poem, the aging wife of an East African settler. In pursuing its meaning, she is forced to refigure her own life, in which she sees herself cut off from her past of family, society, lovers, and landscape. The land that once gratified now terrifies, even as it titillates. Stalking her imagination are primitive energies, either rhino or native restiveness, which turn her reflections from current uncertainties to a past that provides less and less comfort.

In counterpoint to her voice, which is private, tentative, are other voices. They belong to those who listen to the narrator, as we often listen to one another, sometimes intently, sometimes with an ear half-cocked to absorb little more than voice inflections, sometimes rising to her messages, but only grazing their import. In a stellar diagram, their observations are simply other points of light, some may dissipate more quickly than others.

The line that separates the left page from the right is a strip of gauze through which two worlds, text and countertext, see each other.

THE RHINO GATE

I

I skirt the shadows of the rhino gate
for news that tenses. Repetitions, rows
of corn bowing like house boys settled
us but now the murmur of curses
crests like drum beats
beating again, surrounding
the lumbering oxen,
a slow heat their ears
flop on
over umbrellas of dust
rising from their feet,
falling like tablecloth;

        one more day
that overlaps a previous day
       when the old hawker
settled in the valley
of a chair we pushed
from place to place until
it settled here
         where rumor
spikes soft chatter at tea,
sound visible as smoke, full
of speech as folded newspapers
we hesitate to; porch screens
sift the whine from fans and flies
circle slivers of cucumber,
green borders sheltered
by thinly sliced bread.

Their encampment. Gypsies
closing in
on a town, feeling its rind
against them,
rind on rough skin,
a truce,
a comfort.

The rhinoceros has existed for 60 million years and once "stood six meters at the shoulder, was nine meters long and probably weighed 25 tons, or four times as much as today's African bull elephant."

–Bradley Martin

II

There was something before
I imagined a gate to keep us
in, them out; something
before the euphorbia
in the far fields raised thorns
like poison spears, the grasses
tilted in obedience; something
before the rows of wheat slanted
like oars from the horizon,
records moistened in afternoon heat,
mildews of haze over the scribble; something
driven in the heat by fever
trees and thorn scrub,
stilled by the language of breezes.

There are times it never leaves
me; when the flowers are arranged,
tools billeted for the night,
it bulges into the calm,
a pressure in the head,
a boat on the canal
with no name,
that never moves, except to call
out like a chronic ache
I cannot explain.

There are fusses that never end,
saucers that always carry crumbs
on their bottoms.
        And the drums
keep beating like a clock
with no face.

It may have come first in a dream
without faces, the phrase
"rhino gate," letters nudging letters,
r's leaning against h's until they
were there always swelling into repetition
a rush of wind through grass I followed it

By surrendering the scale-like leaves that diminish their moisture, the candelabra euphorbia trees survive in harsh and dry conditions. When the natives want to do away with someone, they dry the euphorbia's poisonous secretions and put it in his beer....The thorn tree is distinguished by powdery yellow bark, small yellowish pom-pon flowers and fine fern-like leaves. "As it grows well near water where mosquitoes breed, it is associated with malaria...."

—Hargreaves

A shrub, the whistling thorn thrives on poorly drained soils or stony ground and is "easily recognized by swollen black galls at the base of larger spines, which are hollow and inhabited by ants."

—Noad/Birnie

"...we seemed to have a lot of oddments, like a side-saddle, a grindstone, an accordion, the Speckled Sussex pullets, an amateur taxidermist's outfit, a pile of enamel basins, a light plow with yokes and chains, rolls of barbed wire . . . ."

—Elspeth Huxley

"I suggested that we should start to teach literacy to those who had not been educated . . . . We could collect handfuls of very fine sand, sieve and heap it in one place and then flatten and smooth it out to the size of a slate. We used sharp-pointed sticks which worked excellently provided the sand was dry and the grain particles were minute enough . . . this all created a firm feeling of unity among us and encouraged our natural resistance . . . ."

—Joseph Mwanga Kariuki

stayed like hunger I did not
understand. It came at the end
of open fields and stopped my world.

We spend more time on the veranda
urging on ivy clutching the stone walk
listening to the fan whining away hours.

We built this house to watch
its aging, our aging, hot breaths
of wind nesting in cracked paint.
In the sun's descending
sacrifice to darkness, purple slashes
the horizon; figures
move across it
from pasture to pasture,

all in the distance,
into darkness.

III

They humped down gray into my childhood,
the rhinos, to a stare I never saw
except over bushes flattened
in books I rubbed
my fingers on to make
them move

and yearned for behind the mbambaras
whenever I felt the flutter
that passed the far fields:
wildebeest curving out empires
in larger and larger arcs, zebras
peering like umpires in a game
no longer played,
stripes frozen into colonial presentation,
heads of giraffes presiding
over treetops swallowing leaffully whole

A deciduous thorny shrub, often used as a fence, the mbambara's inviting leaves are ignored by animals, as they contain bitter tannins.

          –Noad/Birnie

On the move to areas with an abundant supply of food and water, the wildebeest covers great distances, sometimes well over 1000 miles.

There is a wide range of variation among zebras, not merely between types, for example, Birchell and Grevy zebras, but within the same herd.

The habitat chosen by giraffes is "dry open country, covered with bush and acacia; they penetrate into light forest, but never into dense forests."

          –Dorst/Dandelot

shafts of sun
slanting through
like barge poles
breaking against the boughs
spread like a ceremony

so that the sun must have spotted
the rhino grayness like rain,
                    a code
of telegraph keys, as they
moved into shadow,

a mystery I grope at alone,
my him slumped into his wheelchair
like vegetation, ear
like a terrier's the children
leapt at laughing the day
they went off to school up country
screaming at us by beards of corn,
Don't get flustered, don't get flustered
Don't get fantasy in your mustard

What did it mean? I never found
a hint of it in their books or the phrase
"rhino" gate, humped over
everything, a dome,
a gate.

Miro arch at Fondation Maeght

Of shapes such as this, Jacques Dupin has asked, "Of what 'elsewhere' are they native, of what realm of the fantastic are they the voyagers?"

—Guy Weelen

IV

As a girl I dreamed animals
moving across the horizon and filled
the savannas with photos
from magazines, dreams
grown in tall grass
that bundled me

as leopards stalked from side to side
in concrete zoos,
a pendulum,
a timepiece,
like my path
from veranda to smoking house.

My dreams thin with morning
clouds wisping from their mooring,
the rise of coffee beans
brewing curls that bind us to news
three weeks old, a plantation
bought, another sold, another
raid, fourth this month.

                Under our feet
the collapsed blocks
the children have left,
letters we stumble on.

The terrier yelps, worries
his trophy, lion
stuffed with rags, chewed
by children teething.

I look at them now—
lions, leopards, the lot—
settled into sculpture
where we set them
when the sky fell on lawns
like a soft river.

There are no zoos in East Africa, except for one small orphanage in Nairobi. She may be recollecting a childhood visit to a zoo (possibly Regent's Park) or, possibly, something she has read.

—Observer

Near Gilgil: 5,000 acres, including 300-400 acres arable; two fully-equipped dairies, paddocks, good buildings and double-storey house; the whole cost 40,000, will accept 16,000. Voucher 2686

—Kenya Weekly News

"The action so far taken by Government—curfews, collective fines, drafting of additional police to the worst areas—has had no appreciable effect, indeed the situation continues to worsen...."

—Corfield Report

V
Before Bougainvillea
kept the paths, canna poised
like footmen, they appeared, in twos
or threes. The brush withered
around them, collapsed
around their lowered heads. They claimed
a kingdom, a kingdom grew
out of them, out of those horns
slanting like wands to shape a world.

They were a worship our spyglass panned,
nostrils heaving like moving mouths,
mouths skimming the ground
with a blind man's touch,
lips surrounding acacia leaves,
browsing the afternoon into a stillness

they break thundering
over grass at a snapped twig
under boughs that lower
like an invitation,

a past
we giggled at as girls,
imagining oxpeckers pecking
their ears, hopping on the patios
of their backs for picnics.

Beyond the far field
figures shuffle the road,
discs of dust hang
their sharpness in the air
and fall like abandoned coins.

Many East African trees, shrubs, and flowers come from foreign places. Bougain-villea, for example, comes from the Amazon region. It climbs with the aid of the strong, curved spines on its stems, but later on the spines themselves may twine around each other.
            —Lotschert/Beese

There are myths that indicate that both the rhino and the unicorn (of whose exist-ence Aristotle and Pliny were convinced) had horns of enormous strength and the capacity to purify. The unicorn was said to purify water by dipping its horn in it; the rhino's horn is still believed to render some poisons harmless.
            —Bradley Martin

Oxpeckers typically perch on the backs of rhinos and other large game animals "searching for food—ticks and bloodsucking flies"
            —Williams/Arlott

God created Gikuyu and Mumbi
And placed then in Gikuyuland.
They were deceived by the Europeans
And their land was stolen.
            —Mau Mau Song

VI

The sun lowers behind growths
of cloud, its last beams offer
roundness, promise days stretching into rows
of wheat, tips bowing under it,
seducing me down the stairs
led by invitation of jasmine
past the paired rockeries
of agapantha.

          I remembered
the agapantha, how we roused
starlings and rollers, coaxed up
dawns that eased the fever
of dancing lighting night
after night, the breath
of crystal from chandeliers
clinking along high ceilings,
promises bubbling over champagne
toasts
       broken like glass
that can cut so deep and never
heal, the scar out there for gawkers
like a eucalyptus, foreign
and sliced by lightning,

something gone forever;
the fields remain
and spread like my wanting
the tangle where darkness begins
to smooth its boughs,
straighten its branches,
lower its thorns
so that I can feel them as skin,
take them to me
as lovers.

The bark of the jasmine tree is used in parts of Africa to drive away fever; some tribes use the plant as a charm against misfortune; some use the wood for carving.
                                                                —Hargreaves

The 16th century Chinese pharmacist, Li Shih Chen remarked that the major ailments for which rhino horn could be used were, among others, fever and hallucinations.   —Bradley Martin

A tree now common in the highlands of Kenya, the Eucalyptus was originally imported from Australia
                                —OBSERVER

The umbrella thorn or mgunga is an acacia with a flat or umbrella shaped crown. Its "spreading root system makes it a good sand stabiliser, and the pods and leaves are much eaten by game and stock, particularly goats."
                                                —Noad/Birnie

VII

The mist clings to the ridge like teeth
biting off the morning
and releases its grip. The sun,
hung over, lingers over coffee,
a derelict, a last piece
of laundry, a persuasion
that something always remains
unacknowledged, unforgiven
between a last night
cloud and grey horizon promising

nothing, a broken egg
in the sky, a coin
that diminishes to darkness
behind groves where umbrella thorns
assemble like half heads
on an altar.
            They crouch
from light that spears across
our fields and collapses
on ground cover that shelters them.
They name our shapes; they noun
us into stone they surround,
tease with sounds
when we thought the land had sucked
all sound
          and we slope in chairs,
voiceless choirs round a table,
vacant at the end,
no one left to explain,
to tap fingers to the slow waltz
of the moon, to fill a room
with chatter or laughter.

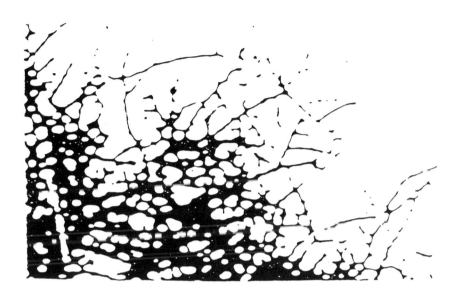

"The warriors also took an oath, *Muma wa Aanake* to bind them before going on a raid. The purpose…was to give those participating a feeling of mutual respect, unity and shared love, to strengthen their relationship, to keep away any bad feelings and to prevent any disputes."

–Joseph Mwangi Kariuki

VIII

It has rained for days,
darts clawing the roof,
flattening the dust on the road.
I imagine thorns flattening
into softness of fur,
rug or house cat—mud
obliterates everything.

Two more planters peeled
from their fields, barnacles
that couldn't be pried loose,
who bowled afternoons away
on a veranda that stretched like highway
until they screened it against raids, packed
for England with photos of grandchildren,
anecdotes of Ribeiro riding down
Victoria Street on a zebra,
remembered when it all
rolled like ocean, when wildebeest
swept across sweeps of plain,
when acacias stood like surprises
we stumbled on—that it was ours,
these fields, the animals
we spared for dreams
and zoos.

The rain has stopped, a silence.
An arena emptied
that insects edge into
with first syllables of chatter.
They stand erect; others rise
to acknowledge and raise battalions
of hum that cover the fields;

"I didn't come to civilize anyone. I came to escape from the slavery one has at home if one doesn't inherit anything. I mean to make a fortune if I can. Then I shall go home and spend it. If that helps to civilize anyone I shall be delighted, but surprised."

"It seemed to go on for ever and ever; beyond each range of hills lay another far horizon; always it was the same, pale-brown grass and bush and thorn-trees, rocky mountains, dark valleys, sunlit plain; there was no break and no order, no road and no town, no places even; just marks on a map which, when you got there, turned out to be merely an expanse of bush or plain exactly like the rest of the landscape."   –Elspeth Huxley

"I have a feeling that this country belongs to us."
                                  –Karen Blixen

". . . the air was pierced by the ceaseless cry of cicadas: how many between here and the Indian Ocean? More, perhaps, even in the few miles around us, than stars that prickled in such millions overhead...."
                                  –Elspeth Huxley

animals tread through it, branches stir
and grunts, muted in rain,
shiver into darkness
like anger

something we forgot about
staring through window panes
counting the slats on the veranda
that needed nails.

IX

The visitors have thinned;
no post for three days; no natives,
only smoke curling up a back road
and yesterday the chatter of Lancasters —
we wait for a burst through the undergrowth.

I have moved the valley
chair to face the fields,
and polished the salvers
to catch the last light.
Its flirtations lancing the porcelain
giraffes upon the piano
keep them there.

The rooom has become smaller.
I tell myself it has given up
space for an extra o
which will not leave my throat.
There are no more corners
to fill with chairs. An album
fills my hand, will not release
its grip. I gloss photos
of children when holidays curbed time
and chimes answered the wind.
Nothing answers the whistle of the kettle.

Rhinos "have a fairly extended vocabulary. They growl, grunt and also emit slight short squeaks, not unlike pigs, quite disproportionate to their size. The most commonly heard is a puffing snort, repeated several times, as an alarm call or when the animal is angry or begins to charge."

–Dorst/Dandelot

"To the minds on both sides in this struggle strange things were happening and our personalities were changing in odd ways."

- Josiah Mwangi Kariuki

"We want co-operation and friendship between races but we do not want that friendship that resembles the friendship of the crocodile and the fish."

–Jomo Kenyatta

It was inside, in this room, children
ran through childhood with tatters
of dolls for their children, wedding
parties went for three days, bursting
into the fields and back roads,
plans were drawn for the first dam,
the local council, the lines
of jacaranda that watched over us
in purple. Nothing happens
in here now, only outside

where darkness drops like an axe,
our only peephole, a sliver
of moon in the western sky.

With hard work and patience, the vision could become real; a house could arise, coffee bushes put down their roots and bloom and fruit, shady trees grow up around a tidy lawn; there was order waiting to be created out of wilderness, a home out of bush, a future from a blank and savage history, a fortune from raw materials that were, as they then existed, of no conceivable value at all...."

—Elspeth Huxley

"I really need my nerve to cope with this eternal balancing on the edge of the abyss...."

—Karen Blixen

X

It is like a day after,
when pipe smoke lingers
and old footpaths conspire
to cover new prints with familiar
heat, beams panning out
the usual comfort.

But it is not the day after;
it is today. The wood slats
under my feet slant
to an edge that racks them.
I roll an olive pit with my tongue,
fasten to the last chapter
of my book and lay it down.
Smoke drifts from the distance
to the far field
like an age that is ending.

Cicada scream runs like a train
that does not stop

until it stops.
We have not heard anything else
not seen anyone along the mud road,
the ruts hardening. This is the way
it comes, daylight
deserting for darkness.
Before we light the lamps we look again,
knowing they are there, escaped
from dreams in skins of leather,
lowering their horns against history
that bridles but cannot restrain.

Routes

NEWS OF GORVACHEV'S OUSTER
ON THE SERENGETI

Acacias remind us by lengthening
shadows that they are there and we
are there, peering at eyes
in the distance, hyena or cheetah
or lion. Cape buffalo stand,
an ancient presentation, stare
out their message: don't use
the outhouse here. No one does.

In the morning we will see
it again: the oppression
of flatness ends; beyond, hill beyond
hill swallows all transport, the frenzy
of a kill, a wildebeest sagging
as if it had nothing to do
with the teeth gripping its throat,
some days later bleached skulls,
no other records
except a few revealing lines
on half-buried stones.
Afternoon heat soothes the high grasses,
flamingoes beat pink against the sky,
starlings line jacaranda branches
that slip into darkness where eyes
candle out their hunger.

A needle
of antenna bleeds news
from the bleached sky:
Gorbachev has left his plain
for the hazard of the high grasses
with little cover
where sun and moon are ignored
and all bridges
lead away from home.

NEW YORK TEACHER AT MOUNT McKINLEY

I know as I shrivel
under them, their ends
will peak through clouds
into my wondering,
probing my slopes of memory.

A cloud coming apart
like a dismembering of alphabet
tells me there is more, voices

      where sound flattens
and tundra continues like a lull
to the horizon's
edge, sloping
here to foothills, before leaping
to a madness of fifteen thousand feet.

      There is a stare
in those boulders, a wall
I try to ignore but cannot
back through. It is

a place I have come from,
a NY barrio classroom
where logarithms
squint judgment into canals
of numbers

where rage carves its height
in graffiti, trash cans
kicked through deserted hours
across a schoolyard. They

make me stare up to mountain sheep
I cannot see and fissures that point
no human way, make me feel
a new comfort with the flat
ground my boots sink into, make me
want to hug cows.

AT THE VILLA DE CALIFORNIA

Lamplight reviews camellia beds
the neighborhood dowagers have weeded,
fingers skimming over soil like snakes
through spikes of grass.
Lazily. The monkey tree still
thickly ribbed, and on the lookout a live oak
savaged, smoldering ash
and a beer bottle left as a flag
at half mast. In shadow
deer step to their own arithmetic.

Each step I take adds to the accounting:
eight kinds of camellia, four cedars,
three palms, two Japanese yews;
mayten, genistafilia, firethorn, trailing
African daisies--all of a party, brought
over oceans for others to see;
scarcely a blade of grass that grows
from its own nativity.

They trekked in from the sea,
parties of four or five
cradling rifles like gifts,
mapped out San Francisco Bay
from the hilltops, swore in Spanish
and returned to their galleons.

They must have wondered,
the Indians watching those boats
before the earth parted
to admit them, their bowls and blankets,
sealing them under a stitchwork of freeways.
They turn in their sleep, heave
up nightmares and earthquakes
that turn up a tree, crack a road.

My hands surround a yew, run like paint
brushes down its bark; they roughen; the paint
does not hold. They do not
belong, my hands, me. All foreign
as this tree which leans
into the blank distances of another
continent.

      Through an open window
an invading guitar twangs to a voice
"You're only a Newfie
in a Calgary hat"

and shafts of lamplight emblazon
the shrubs prickling through
rounded tops, the ends of leaves
pick up a breeze
and I hop across the lawn
like a bandit
on one foot,
a totem
orphaned by a night
it cannot see.

Sharpened Ploughshares

NIGHT TRAIN TO ZAGREB

When gusts spread against the glass
on the Orient Express to Zagreb
snow separates in alphabet,
the vowels clinging to glass,
consonants slipping into drifts.

It must be this way for the howl
to flatten a summons against the pane,
the moaning against the arms
of night pushing it beneath
unbroken meters of the train.

Inside one hand reaches for coffee,
the other sleeve reaches the table
armless, turning in circles
like a pendulum raising questions
as the train turns through the foothills.

It was a Serb. Or was it a Croat?
who came out of a night like this
with candlesticks, something in a bag
and she was there, something
between the doorway and road

or was it the bedroom and kitchen?
And he lowered to her as if
to leave something behind, a kiss
or something more memorable—we
always misunderstand—and her arm

was in the snow, possibly on a night
like this with less to understand
than ice caking on glass
over a broken toothed moan
in alphabet that never shapes.

AT THE JEWISH CEMETERY IN GORA KALWARIA

for Feliks Karpmann
who rebuilt the Jewish cemetery

There are no hills here, the war
flattened them, peeled
the earth like lemon rind releasing
mists that twist through earth

in Hebrew characters
on these stumps of stone;
in neighboring fields
sparrows fly
aimless as tourists.

My mother remembered part of it,
an earlier part: how she clung
to the synagogue floor like a crab
when armies passed through and bullets
splintered the walls; her friend
in blood loosened her grip.

By the cemetery, roadside flowers
rise to attention
by slopes of willow, invading
scrambles of weeds.

I am handed a photo I pluck
to life with my fingers: Jews marching
from one margin to the other, beyond
the photo to Warsaw's ghetto, carrying
flour sacks stuffed with blankets
past a house owned by Borenstein—my mother's

mother?—who lathered her kitchen with laughter
and sang eggs into cake batter.
They carried their sacks
beyond this MEBLE sign
where my uncle baked bread and gossip.
On a poster behind glass, Arnold
Schwarznegger bulges
as predator in black
letters "Soon the hunt will begin."

Here where the cemetery wall stood, they
were lined up, those who hid
in cellars, in tall grass, surfacing
like frogs on marsh lilies
to be plucked by birds with long beaks.
After a few bursts they became
Poland; the cows
in neighboring fields did not
stir.

    And tanks passed over once,
twice, a finale. Headstones lay
like corpses in the camp yard
lathered over with paving tar.

This is what Feliks found,
the town butcher who separated
meat from meadow sounds
into cubes and strips,

who released the stones,
arranged them by height
or alphabet or age.

They blaze like shattered
diamonds on emerald
soft as cloth or meadow,

a gift for anyone
who leaves the road
and walks among stones
that have found their soil
but will not remain silent.

WALDHEIM

A wood to hut in
behind the protecting
tangle of branches
that snows melt around
in early spring.

A memory of emerging
from down
bags, the air
sharp, the sun still
hunkered down under
the horizon.

And the days, days
when hours home
like islands of rain
on polished hoods
in parking lots

while coffee rounds
the rise of campfire
bacon, cream
clotting the surface.

In village fissures below
the mayor's procession
and St. Stephen's feast
run like small rivers
in obedience.

Jewellers on Kaerntnerstrasse
hunch over tangled
springs, squint
them to movement.

At night he mounts
the podium
removes his glasses and skin;
millions applaud
the skull
the dull shine
as it makes speeches
about Austria's place
in the new Europe.

IN OLD PHOTOGRAPHS FROM THE SHTETLACH

the smiles, you realize, are temporary, jokes
hidden from others; you imagine these
shtetl Jews rising from the weight
of their boots passing like clouds
across creases of dirt road, puffs
of life before the draft notice,
before in-laws waved at railway stations,
before the raising of anchors for America,
when foreign soldiers, there for weeks, dragged
an agitator into the woods (no one
saw him again) and burrowed deep holes
into harvests of potatoes and parsnips
while old women screamed in doorways
and roosters made for the barn.

Chickens clucked along shifts
of sunlight to thatched houses,
making a path of the feed;
soliders shook themselves awake—
they they were here to stay—
joked over coffee and soft rolls;
gates opened for hay wagons, the captain
burrowed into the harvest
of the local widow.

It plays back now like film strip
uncut, or paths of flats and sharps
leaping like hurdlers from a score
until they find their path
and rise aimless as bubbles
through an open window,

like days
with no beginning, air full of cluck
and laughter bobbing through kitchens
making paths through windows to open
fields, where soils furrow across
pain, over bodies savaged into silence.

Still it continues, endless
enjambment of fingers and thighs,
leaving a spoor of dried sperm
through centuries, even now

our town beauty
feet in the air like swans'
lowering necks, while circles
of clouds lower
in the sky, the sun
lowers and in her mind necks
of dinosaurs collar around
trees as the earth cracks
to drying skin
and bubbles.

THE OUTPOST

The shadows return to mesas
that confess their passes
in inescapable browns opened
to the long lover's touch
of field glasses
                    recovering
their contours in darkness
that curls against us.

My hand hawks above a plastic bag
and filches something wrapped:
levels of bread surrounding
chopped up off-white—tuna or chicken.
I pretend it is tuna and bite.
It is chicken.

I remember long necks of snow stretching
in woods, on skis, the wind
down, parallel crusts
crumbling under us. I remember
and late Sunday mornings later, sun
warming our toes, watching the kids
colonize kingdoms of lawn that raised
cowlicks across the grass.

Heat haze slips through my head like slow
gas, opens my eyes. How long were they
shut while minutes shredded
to grains of darkness?
A ridge of clay ribs against my hip.
I am not sure which side
of the border I am lying on. I unfold
a map: its creases rearrange
borders. I read poems of Bekri and Laederach,
translate them for the thirtieth
time. Here it is a question of waiting,
the most obscene word in the language,

a harpsichord descent of hurrying notes
or spirals of stairs
that never end,
a hand that reassures
my nakedness with understanding touch
until I forget why I am naked
or what there is to understand,

until I yawn at sunset
blooding the horizon
where there are no human faces.

But I know they are there always
where I cannot see, the other side
of a lip the mountain curls out.
Bombs have splintered it for years
but they come back like a season,
a spring.

      Those who have
their monuments bombed
make a monument of hatred

Who said it? I cannot
remember the mouth, open
like August, the heat dispensing
foreign names; the names grow
higher and fill
the valley like slides of stone
memories of broken thumbs, bodies
hanging by their feet.

They will not be bought
by a rewording of old treaties
cocktail parties or introductions
to Hollywood stars.
The valley will fill;
they will cross it like moonglow
indifferent to our maps, to our poems.

PARLOUR CAR TO ARCHAEOLOGICAL CONVENTION

The window sucks houses
out of darkness, reviews
them in rows slipping
beyond craning necks
into darkness, throws
up blurs of doorways
darkening into mouths that say go
go, we don't need your books.

Settled in armchairs,
scotch and ice,
Time's report of the latest
stabilization in Asia,
three literati
disturb the peace
of coins from Sardis,
resurrect and flip them over
all the way
to Union Station.

While the evening piles a muttering
of house on dark house
over the East River,
we three kings lounge
pressed against glass
with mythologies chinked

to seal out
those kids in puddles
screaming
half naked and alone.

VIETNAM MEMORIAL – CODY, WYOMING

Out of a sky clean
except for buzzards and a hawk
the sun rolls its light
over the names. It is outside
Cody. Few stop here.

The first whisper of wind
levels a tube of sand, highlights
the marble space between Wellfleet
and Wiggins.

A votive coffee can
sprouting geraniums shudders
as two eighteen wheelers
head east to Buffalo.

Three generations after prayers
for rain and buffalo grazed here
I try to imagine the accidents
that lead to this—a couple
of kids at seven in the morning
stepping onto a bus, hand-down
valises, draft notice, unopened
letters making light
of what was to come:

K rations on the edge
of rice paddies, slogging through
marsh or hovering over it.
Going down.

Nothing after this is logged in.

A pick-up awakens
the ground, slits the film
over the names, wind parts
the hair of a rancher on his knees
who sees puffs of dust
building into twisters
that swallow coffee cans, geraniums
lift them so high

that only he can see the boys
dancing with green cows
around a red moon, fiddler
on his stool and a bride
who has just discovered
the first touch of love.

MORNING GOTHIC

It always happens when the action
settles and sags into overstuffed chairs,
when you linger over coffee
or complain about the scrambled eggs,
the white peaking to snow caps
or running into tidal pools,
hoping someone will come through
the door—wife, child, servant, it
never matters—that you hear a knock
and under your eyes is a paper
you cannot read and sweat beads the hands
reaching for glasses you left behind.
A hand grows upon your shoulder
like a strange medal placed too high.
Inside, circles like fingers press you
to the bathroom, but you cannot explain:
words peek from the shelter of your molars
and stay inside; anyway, they are impatient
shifting their eyes to locked doors
and random slips of paper.

The geraniums blurt out yellows
in slanted sun. In window
boxes. Between two boulders
hidden in raincoats
you cannot blurt; you cannot
think of anything
to blurt about.

At a stop light your eyes slip out
of their compound and turn the corner
to each face perched like sculpture, consult
faces of neighbors that have
not slipped across the border:
the tailor's moronic son who joined
the police and became captain in two years

for kicking students in the head—
he said it improved them
and he was for improvement—the mechanic's
son who got thrown out of sculptor's school
and joined the civil guard, pushing
heroin when he could get it; not a face,
nothing on either side
for your wooden hands to frame to, to
recast you as neighbor or aging uncle
or amused bystander. Like them.
Whom you already see in your neighborhood
bar laughing at this old episode.

                    And the longer
list of lawyers, judges, a naval attaché
who will shake your hand, kiss you on each cheek
make it vanish with a wave and broken cough,
insinuating smiles that dress incompetence
in baby blue with apologies to turn this car
home again; but these faces and names low
through telephone wires like official prayers
but come out scrambled, the voices peaked
beyond human hearing and darting
from colored strips like sprinters
on hot coals.

There is nothing left to imagine but the desk
you will sit by, the investigator, bald,
eyeing a cabinet, which you will see
gobbling dossiers, growing a childish face
that understands you and smiles until
you realize that when he reaches for it
he is fondling your funeral stele
even as he offers cigarettes.
You keep a corner of Darkness
at Noon, imagine yourself Rubashov,
knowing that they will do it better
here; they always do it better
when they do it for good causes.

You do not realize the car has stopped
and you are washed by wind as your head
fixes on a bronze door embossed with flowers
and serpents. The king had civil offices
here when civility was triplicate forms
and wax seals, hardly a muted squeal
from the rooms below; next the succession
of generals or was it admirals. You do
not remember but look back and blink
last photographs of a plane tree,
pigeons reflected in the glass
of a rising insurance company
pecking at what the builders have left.

Travelling with Three Eyes

GOING BY RAIL

you soon forget the starting
point, heavy columns, porters
you brush by to dimming light,
the slow movement past monuments you feel
you lived close to, abandoned
cars, as twilight tumbles eyes
of suburban windows you rush by;
your own eyes staring through
interruptions of boxwood groves;
the algebra teacher across you, open
to fractions; your first dinner, a slice
of something whose trip has ended
and some dessert you set aside.

But you remember the prairies—everything
becomes prairie, even waves
of hills succeeding one another, hulks
of mills lengthening in mid day sun
along snake dark water, back hoes
forgotten, and hulls of Ford
pickups rusting in backyards,
their red becomes prairie.

You take suburbs by surprise
bisecting duck paths, grazing
the local zoo where long horn sheep
gaze as though remembering
something else moving beyond
their wired country; you pass
the loading dock of a post office,
two loaders heaving a half dozen bags,

lurch by smoking chimneys,
rear wooden porches; crossings
where locals spar
at the local gym, tap

the light bag of your memory
until you become this countryside
where hung out laundry breathes
you, folds you in each gust,
takes you in—unembarrassed—
a stranger with only loose change
and no official papers.

CHASSIDIM ON THE TGV

And even the schnauzer
hiding behind madame's legs
dismisses them with his eyes
as they run from the leash
of parents and eighteenth
century Polish *shtetlach*.

Rows of eyes rise above
Figaro as though a school
of cat fish had slipped
into their trout stream
surrounding every native hook
with foreign whiskers. Perhaps

they imagine these Chassids
down the long naves they intone in
lurching like local trains,
their sidelocks swinging like railway lamps,
gaucho hats shading the sounds lunging
from their mouths
like panic,
the very joy

of them scrambling
up the dark columns reaching
into darkness
to curlicues of stone

    by a countryside in spring
where bored riders yawn
out fantasies of ewes offering
their rumps like surprises and cardinals
open their beaks for seed, the grey
day blasted by red plumage.

THE NATIVES

They must have been arranged
by a distant hand,
by someone with a feel
for flat backyards.

They hump along steps,
overseeing gutted roads,
reckoning time
by mail truck
and trawler
nudging into dock.

Palm against palm, they sift
sun after sun. Nothing
inside their doors tempts
them now. Even fishing gossip
over eel and cod is worn
and wheels
away the day.

Then, like stock at sundown,
they raise themselves into motion:
a leg extends; another
hesitates after
                to familiar
moves on a checker board; all draw
from each other at the general store;

at the counter pick
licorice that twists like an invention
into a straight line.

VINNY BOOMBATZ

In my barber's stories, Vinny
Boombatz is the offending doctor
or lawyer or whatever we get
to despise as he steals loose
change, spare tires. For some reason you think
yourself awake at two with light coming through
the frizzed boxwoods but Vinny
Boombatz has entered your dreams
squared like a postcard, preparing
a bill to subvert your day
before it starts. You can't remember
whether he has sealed your leaky boiler
or taken apart your carburetor, but you do
know he has screwed it up. You want
righteousness, uninterrupted decades
of judicial robes nodding out judgment,
the martial beat of "Soldiers
of the Queen," no irony
of flaking bark or bleating
trumpet. Vinny

once again survives
the appearance of sunrise, sneaks
into a nest of cloud, makes it
into another day, and you settle
into bed for a few hours
of recovered sleep, conjure
pageantries of geese in flight,
formations spanning continents and Vinny
flying point, wings beating like mad,
honking out something you learned
as a kid and following behind him
you recognize your own beak
honking out Vinny's songs

until you start at 6 in the morning
under a blast of sun, a few clouds,
puffs of underwear, higher
than helium and Vinnie drifting
over them to other continents
out of sight.

FOR A MOMENT or
CONCERNING THE PRONOUN 'IT'

Do you really want
to know how it comes
on mornings when trains
carry the usual crowds

and memos nudge past
other memos and at last
lunch has come and
your question

runs to a stretch
of sun leaning
over rows of desks
like a column

of intentions
that will be taken up
when paper mountains
flatten into plains?

A roof away
girls bathe in sun.
Their laughter slips
into sun. The grass

in the park is cut.
On tracks ledgers slide
back in their darkened
drawers inside.

ONCE IN SOUTH DAKOTA

She took to widowing like fences
stretching white into summer, driving
the red jeep, slipping back
to ancestors or first, gearing up

    to high by rows of corn
    spread out like rib fossils
    blooming from dead breath of dinosaurs,
    and sprouting pompons of silk

    tassels. Tin hulks of Ford wagons
    spread light this Fourth of July.
    It is included; majorettes balance
    it on batons, their pompons

    alive like the bands of color
    on S'dipity's barber pole
    winding like snake coil
    round a tree trunk. A drum beat

    turns the corner by the Bank
    Street Funeral parlor; boys with cowlicks
    blare horns into cumulus clouds
    of sound that pass over blue

    ties and ribbons and the breadths
    of hat rims the Lady's League spreads
    like water flattening under rock
    and engine #4 pokes red surrounded

by green banners and everything
turned like love to the greenest of greens
when they melted to brown
and the corn crapped out in '28.

BUZZARDS BY A DEAD DOG

We pull over by the side of the road,
outside wheels still resting on pavement
and follow an air full of frost and yelps
to four pups, stubby legged but leaping

at buzzards perched in a sycamore,
used to barking, patient as uncles
we've left over thanksgiving dinner
waiting for their brandy and cigars.

At the center is a dog, freshly dead;
whether hit by an eighteen wheeler
or brought to this gully by mange,
we don't walk down to see which.

She says this is how it ought to happen,
in the cold of the year, with nothing left
to chance, and protest nothing more
than mongrels' yelps. There's not much more to make

of this. Sun blaze turns the snow to glints
that cardinals cut in flight. Nothing here
for elegy. We shift back into first
and penetrate Virginia's afternoon.

IN MEMORY OF ELISE ORANGE
WHO STUDIED COMPOSITION

Has it been fifteen or twenty,
God so many, years since Elise Orange
sent her pen windsurfing
through laughter to write? So many
I scarcely remember, but I do
remember she wrote
about her constrictor—there are
people who keep constrictors.

Her name returns swelling.
Not a name I might have picked
at random from a phone book
although as noteworthy as Aqua
or Ochre or Mustard Yellow; before me
again in dresses that lengthen
into outrageous reds and orange. Like her

depositing the weekly mouse,
not the rats you see
stalking sleeping children
on United Fund posters, more
like a windup toy that slips
into your pantry with the cold
around Thanksgiving
and out with spring.

And her pen glides like a snake
and the mouse freezes into sculpture
where it was dropped near particles
of god knows what, I may have imagined
them

and Elise's laughter louder
than any other, deeper, as though
she were dropping into the contralto
of her life; her classmates watching
from tenor ridges

and in quicker than the eye can
see when the eye sees quickly
the mouse is no longer there.

Elise had stopped laughing when she read
the passage; so had we all.

I try to imagine her in cancer
thinned from the blade
of her pen scrawl into the slice
of an obituary, its black blot letters
remain, an afterthought of dark currants
as she passes like memory
into a blankness
pale as sky
serrated as continuity.

DRAGGING IN THE BLUE SHARK

There have been two months of days
like this one, ripening, children
leaning over swollen pilings
to prod starfish and stacks
of lobster traps
to an ocean muster.

Over fingers of rotting pier
a blue shark hangs at the end
of a pulley, its history cut
in water that closed behind it

leaving bubbles of slanted light
where blue bolts over logs
of barracuda, deposits
of grouper.

A trophy measured like other fish
that swim the wrong way,
it would have seemed longer
in the ocean, its own
element, yielding its color
to the dark waters it parted
in endless paths; showing less now
than the squatness of a lion
gate post at Mycenae or a pyramid
of cans at the local
Purity Supreme.

They drag it by the flippers,
drop it in the pick-up
leaving a trail on the gravel,
a hieroglyph of ocean run,
much like a trail of wheelbarrow

hauling earth and other freight,
fronting a '44 Hudson abandoned,
the fender shining green
over spots of salt rust.

THE DIVESTMENT

It is spring, the birds surround you
in adoration as you recognize
public servants and divide
the kingdom, mortgaging country
homes and condominiums
to the keepers of your final years
(you do not know yet that they
will be your keepers) and scraps
to those who will build statues
for children to photograph.

Before two weeks have passed
they pass you in the streets without
a nod, no sign of recognition.

Work on the statues has stopped
and lawyers are dismembering you
holding by holding until you find
yourself with one change of clothes;

not yet like the sockeye salmon fresh
up through fast water and waterfalls
dropping eggs in quiet pools,
coming apart chunk by chunk
until its tail tilts in one shallow
while its dull eye anchors a shredded head
in another;

        not yet, but soon
to come you sense
as questions fall
out of your mouth
in a language like the bunched water
of rapids stretching over stone
flattening into stillness.

Your mind flaps, hands grasp
for a place to watch birds
you could never name but simply
sit under their song over
a wicker basket with hard boiled eggs,
the things of childhood,
but they worry you
into rooms with bedpans and needles
as you mutter syllables; they nod
and smile, putting labels on the scraps
around you so that when you slip
out of a side door you can be picked
out like a '46 Rambler.
On the commode...chest...table, it
doesn't matter, it is
flat, are pictures you trace
with your fingers to make
them real: gowns and square hats,
another of a man and woman.

And after months or weeks or was
it yesterday you hear something
like a name. It distracts
like a loose sign clapping
at shingles and you struggle through
it away over peaks beyond
condor flight and find
some last hints of cloud
dissolving under sun
like scattered alphabet.

THE CIRCUS HORSE

He whips his neck to yank the rope that holds
his canter round the ring's circumference,
his earlier canter down the Bowville Road
past hay stacks peaked by wind or accident
and hedgetops bobbing over countryside
like pompons dancing on the wrists of girls
or swinging on the lead mare's swishing tail.

At clap or wave he rears up on hind legs
and jumps through hoops surrounded by blue flame
as children squeeze their peanuts bunched in bags
and open mouths to circle out his fame
that runs in circles, following the same
galloping through pageantry and parades
five days a week and Wednesday matinees.

Two trainers, equally buffaloed,
stuttered after his leap across the rail
past herds of autos honking down the road
as they jogged after with a water pail
to fifteen other horses tail to tail,
policemens' rolling flesh on cloths of green
patrolling Christmas windows at Filene.

It is not enough that the rope is slack
or that some years have passed since riders
covered the velvet covering on his back
or that its monogram with faded border
presses a claim like truth upon a lover,
over the rippling brook trout spots that stray
with riding into spreading pools of grey.

It is never merely horses breaking gait
or lines that cannot hold the cantering
from turns or sudden tugs, or escapades
that always betray design or demean,

but what comes between: fields of varied green,
the wind lifting the mane up to a crest
and when the last winds die down in evening, rest.

THE EMIGRATION

It was from Zahli that she rose
upon days curled into aromas
of baked bread, and mountains
floated like flat leaves
on waves of August heat;
                    at least
they stretched to magnitude.

But it was the small things
she remembered, salamannders
slithering over whitewashed shutters
losing themselves under leaves
the squash threw out, their pucker
of yellow blossoms

            like the pucker
of Sister Anne at mission school
who hung maps with shapes she called
Europe, Asia, America, and oceans
you could jump across
on one foot, holding a sweet bun. She remembered
the Atlantic, imagined its width—
ten days to cross and the ship
moving at night;

            as she made her way home
along the mountain road, donkey brayed
over patches of anemone; sheep answered.
These were the memories, nothing startling

except what she remembered years later
not sure what was real, what dream, a night
when everything around was black
but sky, stars lighting its dark
circle, fireflies gone
so high from her voice

they could not be recalled,
yet stayed to be stared at
by everything below until everything
was motionless, breath suspended,
and she felt hands around her
insistent as children's fingers
that last a lifetime. Hands so certain
and parental, she wanted them to go,
but could not move from them,

hands that keep you on one side
of the water when boats raise anchor,
and she felt a breath, the only
breath around her, like a reach
of willow branches, a cover
in darkness. Was it a hand or a moment
when wind becomes fingers?

Years later she couldn't remember
but slipped from there like tracks
tracks that so many had made,
an incense she followed
across an ocean. She never
looked back.

Where We Once Were

WINTER FISHERS

The holes in the ice are surrounded
by legs wrapped like chippendales
for shipping, shifting
from side to side as if they belonged
to a better destination,
a warmer plateau. The ice

three feet thick, reassures
like oak, buries everything
beneath our boots. So that we forget
why we are here, baited lines
belonging more to darkness.

What we remember is the wind
that mates us, makes us huddle against
whatever's around—flapping
canvas—call it a tent, it cuts
the wind in half; sterno coffee
conjures up Jamaica, pipe smoke
the slopes of West Virginia.
It only needs wallpaper, a mounted fish
to make this be a home away from home.

But it is down there in darkness
the serious work is carried on
and always was; even before
we knew it, before winter fishers
waited while sudden strokes of fish
tail propelled dark lengths
to food, their eggs, love slugs rolling
below the searching shafts of sunlight
as they outlined shoreline and rock
like borders, opening and closing
mouths designed for browsing
accepting the luxury of tangents
only in warm twilights, through still water,
rising for the waterlogged dragonfly.

But now one strikes at this mouthful
which should not be here, hanging
against current and common sense—
outside its boundary like a surprise
that surprises it   and the line
that now bobs the stiffness from its pole
from the clothesful of arms and legs
around the hole, fingering lengths
of line, the tug drawing him further
further to that world
he hovers over and all he will know of it—
a manhole of indescribable darkness
and the blast of light
the leaping fish will enter.

THE CARP IN FAIGE'S BATH

Transoms, faceless door knobs
wobbling, hinges stiff as grenadiers,
they gave me terror before I gave
them names that Sunday, week
before Aunt Faige's seder
when carp and pike swam
into balls of gefilte fish,
an afternoon that lingered
long after knaidels
and cousins left the table.

The knob was a mystery, a toy
that didn't work, turn as I might,
and getting out dwindled like a transom
closing for the night. Voices

of uncles and aunts lobbed advice
through cracks as I stared at the tank,
that stone head on the wall,
baldness beaded with water,
presiding over me. I yanked its chain leash
and watched it flush fishless
waterfalls, whooshing like an animal,
a Niagara falling always coming
into that round of porcelain white

with the bulb hanging from wire
frozen in cloths of light,
toothbrushes paralyzed
in their ivory stands, and paste
stuck to stubs of bristle.

Below the carp swam
swifter circles, darting
at angles as if trumpets
had sounded and magic were about
to split the porcelain
and open its way to larger waters.

WILDFLOWERS

Campers walk the gravel path at night
and pass a lighted window, a vase
of wildflowers in it, circled
from the dark, as though sun surrounded
the glass and left
it blossoms the lightness
of butterfly wings,

yellows golding out
the purples of night,

passing through them
to gloss the skull caps
of dew on each head
of bee flower.

They watch and shadow
plays like fleets of minnows
over their toes,
nibbling at the poles
growing out of sandals—too
stiff for play or love.

Darkness hardens
and the beam
turns back
through the glass
running like a lechery
over the spines
of ferns and cornflowers.

FROM THE ALBUM

It is over now—the TV, evening
snacks; the lights turned down.
The daylight has spent itself
on cornflowers and lupin, weights us
under meadow scent to sleep.

Crossword puzzles folded on the floor
release letters that you breathe
against me, like land sails on sand
driven by drifts of air

         as light
stripes our bodies through
the slatted door.

        And we open
to a stretch of forest floor
where blue foxes edge their way along
lines of light that slat
through stands of pine.

Rising from sleep and each other's arms,
I find the street gone narrow,
its oracles not to be believed.

WEDDING POEM

There are caves I would not walk
into with a flashlight; the light
flashing paths along the wall would
remind us that we'd left whole blocks
of light breaking a first rose
on burnt oranges, reds and golds,
chrysanthemums sheltered in a vase.

And even if we left to pad foot
by foot by walls where walls breathe
water and water stands in pools
as clear as ice, we would end
by imagining October sun
bypassing our coffee cups to browse
on carpet flowers for its holiday.

It may be early to leave first light
like kids on a first fishing trip
huddled in the bottom of a boat
venturing from a world we know
less with our minds than with our hands.
Still, this cave opens like an invitation
that is dumb until we say we'll come.

BORDERS OF A CANADIAN CHILDHOOD WINTER

In that winter when the ground froze
sprawled stacks of wood solid
for 94 days until March
loosened them, we kept the feeders
full and watched the birds—
sparrows mainly— spread hulls
like pimples on the snow,
a kind of avian Mamma Leone's
where every plate oozed sauce beyond the edge
(my mother's table also comes to mind—
soup sloshing tidal waves of peas
to the bowl's gilt brim of seigniorial gowns).

We hid our faces under parkas' hoods
sheltered by forts of snow, lobbing snowballs
over forts we hadn't built, white
insects that never left our streets
and stayed the winters. Sometimes we stayed
inside hinging together puzzles piece by piece
laying borders out like provinces
building Tarzan whose hair was always blue
and Captain Marvel who flew and never fell

while rhododendrons tightened into hoods,
tightened their veins, and all
main street tightened its veins to keep
the glacial air out, veins tightened
around the whole countryside

until they swelled
and we accepted the rise of tulips,
geese that honked for two days
but never dropped onto the green
despite almanacs and local prophecy,

the only year the county won four ribbons
in the fair, corn came
in two weeks early
and Hummie Luff blocked forty-seven shots,
one with his nose, that kept
him humming into story books.

And that was the year that I discovered wrens.

SIGNAL EDITIONS